WATFORD

This book belongs to

Age

Favourite player

Prediction of Watford's final position this season

Prediction of Barclays Premier League winners this season

Prediction of Barclays Premier League runners-up

Prediction of FA Cup winners this season

Prediction of Capital One Cup winners this season

Written by twocan

Contributors: Steve Scott, Luke Weston, Jonathan North, Alex Urse, Rob Mason

A TWOCAN PUBLICATION

©2015. Published by twocan
under licence from Watford FC.

ISBN 978-1-909872-66-0

PICTURE CREDITS
Alan Cozzi, Action Images, Press Association.

£8

PUMA #FOREVER

Contents

WATFORD

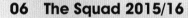

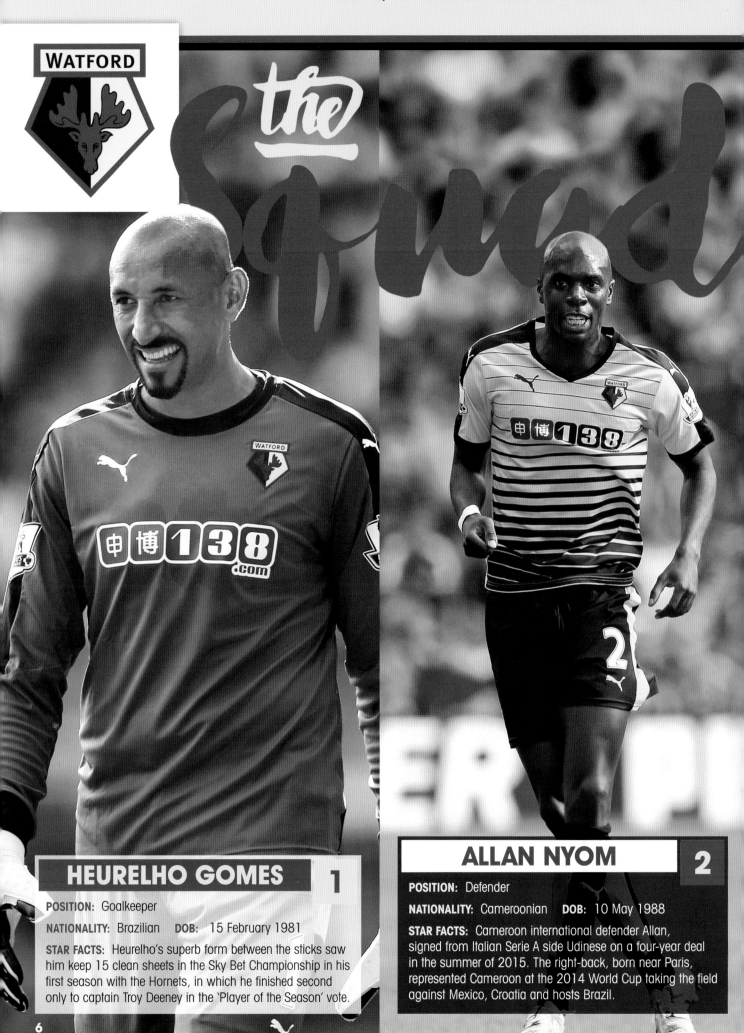

WATFORD

the Squad

HEURELHO GOMES | 1

POSITION: Goalkeeper

NATIONALITY: Brazilian   **DOB:**   15 February 1981

STAR FACTS: Heurelho's superb form between the sticks saw him keep 15 clean sheets in the Sky Bet Championship in his first season with the Hornets, in which he finished second only to captain Troy Deeney in the 'Player of the Season' vote.

ALLAN NYOM | 2

POSITION: Defender

NATIONALITY: Cameroonian   **DOB:**   10 May 1988

STAR FACTS: Cameroon international defender Allan, signed from Italian Serie A side Udinese on a four-year deal in the summer of 2015. The right-back, born near Paris, represented Cameroon at the 2014 World Cup taking the field against Mexico, Croatia and hosts Brazil.

MIGUEL BRITOS — 3

POSITION: Defender

NATIONALITY: Uruguayan   **DOB:** 17 July 1985

STAR FACTS: Experienced Uruguayan defender Miguel, joined the Hornets from Italian side Napoli. He played more than 100 times for the Serie A outfit between 2011 and 2015, and during his stay won the Coppa Italia twice and the Super Cup once.

JOEL EKSTRAND — 6

POSITION: Defender

NATIONALITY: Swedish   **DOB:** 4 February 1989

STAR FACTS: Since joining from Udinese Joel had been a regular in the Hornets' starting XI, until a knee injury suffered against Ipswich in March cut short his promotion-winning 2014/15 campaign and ruled him out of the early part of Watford's Premier League season.

SEBASTIAN PRODL — 5

POSITION: Defender

NATIONALITY: Austrian   **DOB:** 21 June 1987

STAR FACTS: Sebastian joined Watford from Werder Bremen on a five-year deal in June 2015. He appeared in both the Champions League and the Europa League during his seven years at the Weserstadion, as well as winning the German Cup in 2009. The 6ft 4in stopper is an established Austrian international and collected his 50th cap shortly after signing for the Hornets.

JOSE MANUEL JURADO — 7

POSITION: Midfielder

NATIONALITY: Spanish   **DOB:** 29 June 1986

STAR FACTS: Attacking midfielder Jose, completed a move to Watford from Spartak Moscow ahead of the 2015/16 Premier League season. The Spaniard, who was a product of Real Madrid's youth setup, made a handful of appearances for Los Blancos before moving to rivals Atletico Madrid in 2006. He played 115 times for Atletico, including 64 outings and nine goals in 2009/10 as the side managed by current Watford Head Coach Quique Sanchez Flores stormed to Europa League glory.

VALON BEHRAMI

8

POSITION: Midfielder

NATIONALITY: Swiss   **DOB:** 19 April 1985

STAR FACTS: The Yugoslavia-born midfielder completed a move back to the Premier League from Hamburg, after previously spending two-and-a-half top-flight years with West Ham United between July 2008 and January 2011. Internationally, Behrami has over 50 caps for his country, and has made the Swiss squad at three FIFA World Cup tournaments and UEFA Euro 2008.

TROY DEENEY

9

POSITION: Striker

NATIONALITY: English   **DOB:** 29 June 1988

STAR FACTS: Troy firmly etched his name in the Watford FC history books in 2014/15, becoming the first player in the club's history to hit 20-plus goals in three successive seasons, with a 21-goal haul. The Birmingham-born striker captained the Hornets to Premier League promotion, and took home both the Player and Players' Player of the Season awards.

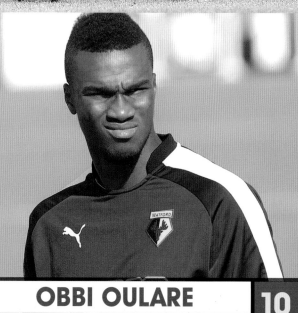

OBBI OULARE

10

POSITION: Striker

NATIONALITY: Belgian   **DOB:** 8 January 1996

STAR FACTS: Obbi was part of the Club Brugge squad that faced Manchester United in the Champions League qualifying stages, just weeks before his switch to Watford on transfer deadline day at the start of September. The Belgium U21 international came through the Academy ranks at Lille in France, where fellow countrymen Eden Hazard and Divock Origi also graduated.

WATFORD

the Squad

LLOYD DOYLEY   12

POSITION: Defender

NATIONALITY: Jamaican   **DOB:** 1 December 1982

STAR FACTS: Lloyd, the Hornets' longest-serving player, has been with Watford since the age of nine. He now has more than 400 Watford games under his belt and has moved into fifth place in the Hornets' all-time appearance list.

RENE GILMARTIN   13

POSITION: Goalkeeper

NATIONALITY: Irish   **DOB:** 31 May 1987

STAR FACTS: Rene returned to Vicarage Road in August 2014. The 6' 6" goalkeeper had previously made seven appearances for the Hornets between 2010 and 2012. After leaving Watford, Rene spent a year with Plymouth Argyle before returning to Ireland with St Patrick's Athletic.

JUAN CARLOS PAREDES   14

POSITION: Defender

NATIONALITY: Ecuadorian   **DOB:** 8 July 1987

STAR FACTS: Attack-minded, versatile defender Juan Carlos, arrived at Vicarage Road after impressive performances for his country at the 2014 FIFA World Cup in Brazil, in which he completed 90 minutes in each of La Tricolor's group matches as they narrowly missed out on the last-16.

9

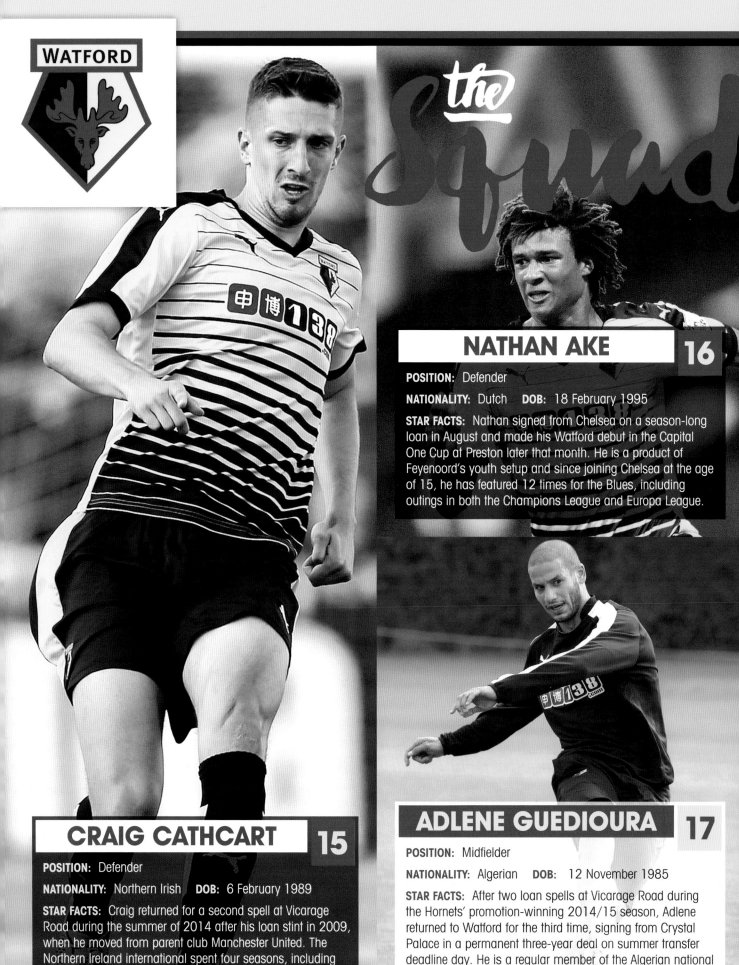

WATFORD

the Squad

NATHAN AKE — 16

POSITION: Defender

NATIONALITY: Dutch   **DOB:** 18 February 1995

STAR FACTS: Nathan signed from Chelsea on a season-long loan in August and made his Watford debut in the Capital One Cup at Preston later that month. He is a product of Feyenoord's youth setup and since joining Chelsea at the age of 15, he has featured 12 times for the Blues, including outings in both the Champions League and Europa League.

CRAIG CATHCART — 15

POSITION: Defender

NATIONALITY: Northern Irish   **DOB:** 6 February 1989

STAR FACTS: Craig returned for a second spell at Vicarage Road during the summer of 2014 after his loan stint in 2009, when he moved from parent club Manchester United. The Northern Ireland international spent four seasons, including one in the Premier League, with Blackpool, where he made over 100 appearances for the Seasiders.

ADLENE GUEDIOURA — 17

POSITION: Midfielder

NATIONALITY: Algerian   **DOB:** 12 November 1985

STAR FACTS: After two loan spells at Vicarage Road during the Hornets' promotion-winning 2014/15 season, Adlene returned to Watford for the third time, signing from Crystal Palace in a permanent three-year deal on summer transfer deadline day. He is a regular member of the Algerian national side, and made three appearances at the 2010 World Cup in South Africa.

VICTOR IBARBO   19

POSITION: Forward

NATIONALITY: Colombian   **DOB:** 19 May 1990

STAR FACTS: Colombian international Victor arrived from Roma on a season-long loan on transfer deadline day at the start of September. The versatile 6ft 2in forward can play anywhere across the front-line and with his power and pace, he should provide a real threat. He played three times at the 2014 World Cup in Brazil, as his country made their way to the quarter-finals.

STEVEN BERGHUIS   20

POSITION: Striker

NATIONALITY: Dutch   **DOB:** 19 December 1991

STAR FACTS: Steven become a Watford player after joining from Dutch side AZ Alkmaar ahead of the 2015/16 Premier League campaign. The winger, who is comfortable playing on either flank, scored 11 goals in 22 league games in 2014/15 and his impressive form for AZ earned him his first international call-up to the full Netherlands squad ahead of their Euro 2016 qualifier against Latvia in June 2015.

IKECHI ANYA   21

POSITION: Midfielder

NATIONALITY: Scottish   **DOB:** 3 January 1988

STAR FACTS: Ikechi, renowned for his skill, speed and versatility, joined from Granada, originally on loan in July 2012, before signing a permanent deal prior to the 2013/14 campaign. Although eligible to play for England (through residence), Nigeria (through his father) or Romania (through his mother), he chose to play international football for Scotland. His debut came against Belgium in September 2013 and he scored his first goal in the following 2-1 win in Macedonia.

ALMEN ABDI | 22

POSITION: Midfielder

NATIONALITY: Swiss   **DOB:** 21 October 1986

STAR FACTS: Almen joined Watford from Udinese in the summer of 2012 on loan and the cultured midfielder made an instant impact at Vicarage Road, winning the 2012/13 Player of the Year award. Almen's career began at FZ Zurich, where he made over 100 appearances in six years in Switzerland, before a short spell at Le Mans in France, followed by two years in Italy.

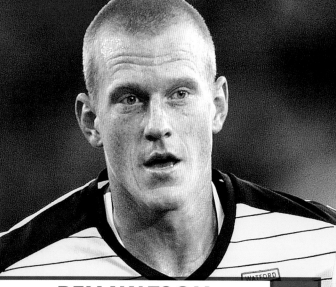

BEN WATSON | 23

POSITION: Midfielder

NATIONALITY: English   **DOB:** 9 July 1985

STAR FACTS: Ben is now a permanent fixture at Vicarage Road after initially joining on loan from Wigan Athletic in January 2015. He played 133 games during his six years with the Latics - his best moment being his dramatic injury time winning goal in the 2013 FA Cup Final against Manchester City.

ODION IGHALO | 24

POSITION: Striker

NATIONALITY: Nigerian   **DOB:** 16 June 1989

STAR FACTS: Odion became a permanent member of Watford's squad in October 2014, having initially signed on a one-year loan from Udinese just three months previous. The striker arrived in England having been on loan at Granada, from parent club Udinese, since signing for the Little Zebras in 2008.

WATFORD

the Squad

JOSE HOLEBAS 25

POSITION: Defender

NATIONALITY: Greek **DOB:** 27 June 1984

STAR FACTS: International Jose, signed from Italian Serie A 2014/15 runners-up AS Roma in the summer of 2015, ahead of the Hornets' return to the Premier League. He has a wealth of top-level experience, approaching 30 games for his country as well as 23 Champions League appearances.

BERNARD MENSAH 26

POSITION: Striker

NATIONALITY: English **DOB:** 29 December 1994

STAR FACTS: Bernard is one of Watford Academy's success stories. The striker managed 14 goals in 19 appearances for the Golden Boys' U18 side during the 2012/13 season, and joined the Hornets' first-team squad at the start of pre-season training in July 2013. He made his professional debut in November 2013, at just 18 years of age.

ESSAID BELKALEM 27

POSITION: Defender

NATIONALITY: Algerian **DOB:** 1 January 1989

STAR FACTS: Essaid played ten times for the Hornets during an injury-hit 2013/14, making his debut in front of the Hornets' faithful in a 2-0 win against AFC Bournemouth in the Capital One Cup. Watford made the loan move permanent in June 2014, before the Algerian defender went to the 2014 World Cup in Brazil, making three appearances for his national side.

the Squad

CONNOR SMITH 28

POSITION: Midfielder

NATIONALITY: Irish **DOB:** 18 February 1993

DID YOU KNOW? Connor, a product of the Watford Academy, joined the Hornets' professional ranks for the first time in 2011/12 and made his professional debut in August 2012 away to Crystal Palace, coming on as a substitute. He has also been capped at U17, U19 and U21 levels by his native Ireland.

JORELL JOHNSON 30

POSITION: Defender

NATIONALITY: English **DOB:** 2 January 1996

STAR FACTS: Jorell is a commanding central defender who joined the Watford FC Academy in May 2007 and captained the U18s during his two years as a scholar at Vicarage Road, before signing professional terms in May 2014.

ETIENNE CAPOUE 29

POSITION: Midfielder

NATIONALITY: French **DOB:** 11 July 1988

STAR FACTS: A Watford newcomer this season, Etienne joined the Hornets from Tottenham Hotspur in July for a club record transfer fee. He signed for Spurs from French side Toulouse, where he played nearly 200 matches after progressing through their youth ranks. He has played seven times for his country, scoring once, in a 3-1 victory over Belarus during qualification for the 2014 FIFA World Cup.

TOMMIE HOBAN 31

POSITION: Defender

NATIONALITY: Irish **DOB:** 24 January 1994

STAR FACTS: Academy product Tommie, has now made over 50 Watford appearances and is a regular in the Golden Boys' back-line. He has represented Ireland at U17 level, captained the U19s and played for the U21s.

LLOYD DYER 33

POSITION: Midfielder

NATIONALITY: English **DOB:** 13 September 1982

STAR FACTS: Lloyd completed a move to Vicarage Road in July 2014. The wide player has a wealth of experience, having played over 200 games for Leicester City where he hit 10 goals in the Foxes 2013/14 Championship title-winning campaign.

ALESSANDRO DIAMANTI 32

POSITION: Midfielder

NATIONALITY: Italian **DOB:** 2 May 1983

STAR FACTS: Italian international Alessandro, arrived at Vicarage Road on a season-long loan from Chinese side Guangzhou Evergrande, just after the start of the 2015/16 Premier League campaign. The technically gifted playmaker who has previous Premier League experience with West Ham United, has represented his country 17 times.

GIEDRIUS ARLAUSKIS 34

POSITION: Goalkeeper

NATIONALITY: Lithuanian **DOB:** 1 December 1987

STAR FACTS: The experienced shot-stopper arrived at Vicarage Road having won the Romanian title with Steaua Bucharest in 2014/15. At 6ft 3in, Giedrius has European pedigree, playing in the Champions League and the Europa League for Steaua, Rubin Kazan and Unirea Urziceni. Arlauskis has 20 caps for Lithuania and kept goal against England in the Euro 2016 qualifier at Wembley in March 2015.

JOSH DOHERTY 35

POSITION: Midfielder

NATIONALITY: Northern Irish **DOB:** 15 March 1996

STAR FACTS: Josh made his first-team debut as a substitute against Huddersfield on the last day of 2013/14, just a couple of weeks before earning his maiden pro contract. He gained a reputation at U18 level as a set-piece specialist, and showed great character on putting his name forward for spot-kick duty when Watford were awarded a late penalty just ten minutes into his Huddersfield debut, an offer eventual taker and scorer Troy Deeney politely declined.

ALEX JAKUBIAK 36

POSITION: Striker

NATIONALITY: English **DOB:** 27 August 1996

STAR FACTS: After impressing for the U18s, Alex was loaned to Conference side Braintree Town, where he scored a stunning long-range strike, minutes into his debut in a 3-0 win over Wrexham. Six days after making his Watford debut, at home to Huddersfield Town in the final game of the 2013/14 season, he signed his first pro contract. In August 2014, he moved on loan to League Two side Oxford United and scored his first goal for the Us on his first start. Then in November 2014, he joined League Two side Dagenham & Redbridge and again, scored on his debut.

ALFIE YOUNG 37

POSITION: Defender

NATIONALITY: English **DOB:** 3 February 1997

STAR FACTS: Alfie joined up with the Hornets' squad after signing his first professional contract in the summer. The 18-year-old defender, who is a product of Watford's Academy, captained the Hornets' Under-18s last season, while also featuring for the Under-21s.

WATFORD

the Squad

MAHLONDO MARTIN — 38

POSITION: Midfielder

NATIONALITY: English   **DOB:** 15 October 1996

STAR FACTS: Mahlondo was another Academy graduate to be rewarded with a professional contract during the summer. A talented left-sided wide-man, the 18-year-old impressed with a series of impressive U18 and U21 displays last term.

DENNON LEWIS — 39

POSITION: Striker

NATIONALITY: English   **DOB:** 9 May 1997

STAR FACTS: Dennon put pen to paper on his first professional deal during the summer of 2015. He joined the club's Academy at Under-11 level, progressed through the ranks and was heavily involved within the Under-18 and Under-21 squads last season. Lewis, who can play on either wing or up front, netted 18 times for the Under-18s last term and gained valuable first-team experience in the pre-season friendly fixtures.

GEORGE BYERS — 40

POSITION: Midfielder

NATIONALITY: Scottish   **DOB:** 29 May 1996

DID YOU KNOW? Scotland youth international George, joined Watford's Academy at the age of seven, signed his first professional contract during the summer of 2014 and made his professional debut as a late substitute during the Hornets' 5-0 win over Charlton in January 2015.

MEET YOUR RIVALS

ARSENAL

GROUND: Emirates Stadium **CAPACITY:** 60,432
MANAGER: Arsène Wenger **NICKNAME:** The Gunners
DID YOU KNOW: Arsenal are one of the most successful clubs in English football, they have won 13 First Division and Premier League titles and a joint record 11 FA Cups.

ASTON VILLA

GROUND: Villa Park **CAPACITY:** 42,788
MANAGER: Tim Sherwood **NICKNAME:** The Villans
DID YOU KNOW: Villa currently hold the record number of league goals scored by any team in the English top-flight - 128 goals were scored in the 1930/31 season.

BOURNEMOUTH

GROUND: The Vitality Stadium **CAPACITY:** 11,700
MANAGER: Eddie Howe **NICKNAME:** The Cherries
DID YOU KNOW: They won the Championship last season and were promoted to the Barclays Premier League for the first time in their history.

CHELSEA

GROUND: Stamford Bridge **CAPACITY:** 41,798
MANAGER: José Mourinho **NICKNAME:** The Blues
DID YOU KNOW: Chelsea are the only London club to have won the UEFA Champions League.

CRYSTAL PALACE

GROUND: Selhurst Park **CAPACITY:** 26,309
MANAGER: Alan Pardew **NICKNAME:** The Eagles
DID YOU KNOW: The club has an American bald eagle called Kayla as the club mascot, which flies from one end of the stadium to the other at every home game.

EVERTON

GROUND: Goodison Park **CAPACITY:** 40,221
MANAGER: Roberto Martinez **NICKNAME:** The Toffees
DID YOU KNOW: Everton have a very close rivalry with neighbours Liverpool. Goodison Park is only 0.6 miles from Liverpool's Anfield.

LEICESTER CITY

GROUND: King Power Stadium **CAPACITY:** 32,262
MANAGER: Claudio Ranieri **NICKNAME:** The Foxes
DID YOU KNOW: The Foxes were rooted to the bottom of the table on Christmas Day 2014, but escaped the drop in dramatic fashion, winning seven of their last nine games.

LIVERPOOL

GROUND: Anfield **CAPACITY:** 45,522
MANAGER: Brendan Rodgers **NICKNAME:** The Reds
DID YOU KNOW: The Reds have won more European titles than any other English club - five European Cups, three UEFA Cups and three UEFA Super Cups.

MANCHESTER CITY

GROUND: Etihad Stadium **CAPACITY:** 55,100
MANAGER: Manuel Pellegrini **NICKNAME:** The Citizens
DID YOU KNOW: City hold the record for the fewest goals scored at home in a regular Premier League season - ten in 2006/07.

TOP 3: Midfielders

A cultured left-sided player, Kenny Jackett was in sight of the club appearance record when injury ended his playing career at the age of 28.

Jackett was part of Graham Taylor's side that won promotion to the First Division, and he also played in the club's only appearance in an FA Cup Final back in 1984. He won 31 full Welsh caps and went on to coach Watford's first-team. He then became assistant to Ian Holloway at QPR but left to take the top job at Swansea. After a brief stint as Man City's reserve team manager he took over the helm at Millwall in November 2007. Jackett is the current manager of SkyBet Championship side Wolves.

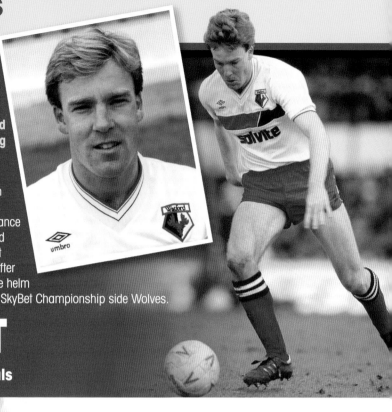

KennyJACKETT

Watford 1980-1990: 428 Games · 34 Goals

GaryPORTER

Watford 1982-1997
470 Games · 46 Goals

Watford legend and third highest all-time appearance maker Gary Porter was recently inducted into the club's Hall of Fame after a fantastic career at Vicarage Road, where he made 472 appearances and scored 56 goals.

After first going on trial at the club aged 11, Porter joined fully at 16 in 1982, and enjoyed 15 years with the Hornets before leaving at 31. After leaving the Hornets in 1997, Porter returned North, playing for Walsall and Scarborough, before finishing his career at Boston United. Porter also played 12 times for England's Under-21s during the 1980s.

JohnBARNES

Watford 1981-1987:
296 Games · 85 Goals

John Barnes' rise from park football to Watford star, coupled with sumptuous natural ability, made him a crowd favourite at Vicarage Road, after his debut aged just 17.

Barnes went on to play just under 300 games for the Hornets, which included playing an influential part in the team of 1981/82 which were promoted to the top-tier, completing a six-year rise from the fourth division to the top-tier, under Graham Taylor. Internationally, he played just under 80 times for England, scoring a wonder goal against Brazil in 1984, when he dribbled past numerous defenders before rounding Roberto Costa to score.

DRILLS: Fitness

WATFORD

You will need cones or markers, a ball and a friend!

Shuttle runs are a great fitness training exercise to help build speed, stamina, acceleration and endurance. Adding a football helps players control the ball at top speeds and when the body is tired.

Remember to swap roles with your friend so you both get a chance to work on your fitness!

EASY...

Set up a line of 6-8 cones 5 metres apart. To begin with, run from the first cone to the second cone and back again. Next, run to the second cone and back again.

Continue to do this until you have completed a run to the final cone.

HARD...

Now, add a football into the mix!

Dribble from the start to the first cone, turn with the ball, pass back to your friend and then sprint back to the start. Your friend should stop the ball at the start where you will gain possession and dribble to the second cone.

Repeat this process for each of the cones.

START

HARDER...

There are many ways you can increase the difficulty level.

Have your friend throw the ball to you as you're running back to the start. You will have to work to bring the ball under control, bring it back to the start and dribble on to the next cone - work on chest traps, thigh traps as well as traps with the feet.

As you improve, try and work faster.

Can you invent some variations to make it harder?

Can you match each of these mascots to the Clubs they support?

MANCHESTER UTD · WEST HAM UTD · SUNDERLAND · ARSENAL · NORWICH CITY · SHEFFIELD WEDNESDAY · LEEDS UTD · BIRMINGHAM CITY

WATFORD

A. MASCOT:
CLUB:

The Big

B. MASCOT: CLUB:

Match

C. MASCOT: CLUB:

D. MASCOT: CLUB:

E. MASCOT: CLUB:

F. MASCOT: CLUB:

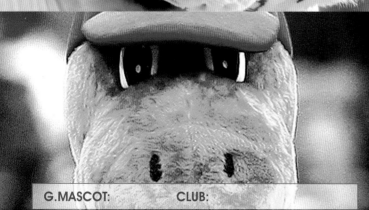

G. MASCOT: CLUB:

H. MASCOT: CLUB:

22

ANSWERS ON PAGE 62

Ikechi**ANYA**

21

Crowd PLEASERS

WATFORD

first half OF THE SEASON

WATFORD V SWANSEA CITY

Swansea are the first Welsh team to play in the Premier League. True or false?

5. ANSWER

EVERTON V WATFORD

Name Everton's 6'3" American shot-stopper.

1. ANSWER

NEWCASTLE UNITED V WATFORD

Who is the owner of Newcastle United?

6. ANSWER

WATFORD V WEST BROMWICH ALBION

What bird is on the WBA badge?

2. ANSWER

WATFORD V SOUTHAMPTON

In what year did the Saints lift the FA Cup?

3. ANSWER

WATFORD V CRYSTAL PALACE

What is Crystal Palace's nickname?

7. ANSWER

MANCHESTER CITY V WATFORD

Where was Manchester City's manager, Manuel Pellegrini, born?

4. ANSWER

BOURNEMOUTH V WATFORD

Name the Cherries' Russian owner.

8. ANSWER

WATFORD V ARSENAL

What colour is Arsenal's away kit this season?

9. ANSWER

WATFORD V LIVERPOOL

How many times have Liverpool won the FA Cup?

17. ANSWER

STOKE CITY V WATFORD

Stoke City are based in which English county?

10. ANSWER

WATFORD V MANCHESTER UNITED

The Red Devils were formed in 1878 as who?

13. ANSWER

CHELSEA V WATFORD

What is the capacity of Stamford Bridge?

18. ANSWER

WATFORD V WEST HAM UNITED

What is West Ham United's theme song?

11. ANSWER

ASTON VILLA V WATFORD

Who managed Aston Villa before Tim Sherwood?

14. ANSWER

WATFORD V NORWICH CITY

Who was City's promotion-winning captain last season?

15. ANSWER

WATFORD V TOTTENHAM HOTSPUR

What does Spurs' Latin motto 'Audere est Facere' mean?

19. ANSWER

LEICESTER CITY V WATFORD

Leicester City are known as the Ferrets. True or false?

12. ANSWER

SUNDERLAND V WATFORD

Who is the Black Cats' manager?

16. ANSWER

TOP 3: Defenders

John McClelland signed for Watford in 1984 from Scottish side Glasgow Rangers, before going on to make over 230 appearances for the club in a five-year spell.

McClelland was well known amongst the Watford faithful for his coolness under pressure and exceptional leadership skills. During his time with the Hornets, his consistently excellent performances earned him a place at the 1986 World Cup with Northern Ireland, while he also captained his country on numerous occasions. Renowned for his ungainly running style, McClelland also possessed incredible speed and scored three goals during his spell at Vicarage Road.

JohnMcCLELLAND

NigelGIBBS

A dependable and loyal right-back, and a massive fans' favourite, Gibbs made his debut for the Golden Boys in a UEFA Cup tie against Sparta Prague in 1983.

Gibbs was loved by all at Vicarage Road for his tough tackling, determination and his exceptional positional play, and deservedly won the Watford Player of the Season award at the end of the 1991/92 season. Unfortunately, he suffered a career-threatening injury in 1993 and was released in 1996. But fortunately for both Gibbs and Watford, he stayed with the club, joining them for pre-season training and ended up signing a new contract. Gibbs served Watford as a player for a remarkable 20 years, making his final appearance for the club in April 2002. In total, Gibbs made 491 appearances for the Hornets and scored seven goals in the process.

WilfROSTRON

Rostron began his Watford career as a left-winger having signed for the club from Sunderland in 1979. However, Graham Taylor soon saw Rostron's potential at left-back and he went on to make over 400 appearances for the Hornets during a ten year stay at Vicarage Road.

During his time at Watford, Rostron went on to captain the Golden Boys and made 40 consecutive FA Cup appearances, before suspension unfortunately deprived him of the opportunity to lead his side out at Wembley for the 1984 final. Rostron was an integral part of the side that won promotion to Division One in 1981/82, before winning Watford Player of the Season at the end of the following campaign in the English top flight. Rostron also chipped in with an impressive 30 goals during his time with Watford.

DRILLS: Heading

WATFORD

Have your mates form a circle around you, everyone facing you. You have the ball.

EASY

Throw the ball towards the other players' heads in turn, as if they are going to head the ball.

While the ball is in the air, shout 'HEAD' or 'CATCH' to whoever you are directing the ball to. The player must then quickly react to your command and perform the task you have shouted.

If you yelled 'HEAD' the player must head the ball back to you.

If you yelled 'CATCH' the player must catch the ball and return it.

If a player performs the wrong task, that player sits and only standing players are still in the game. The last player standing wins the round.

HARD

To make this drill more difficult, have the players do the opposite task to what you have shouted, e.g. if you shout 'CATCH' they must 'HEAD' the ball.

Also start throwing the ball to players randomly, keeping everyone on their toes as they don't know whose turn will be next!

> This drill is supposed to be fun!
> You will be working on your heading and reaction skills without even realising it!

> Make sure to take turns being the player in the middle!

HARDER

To develop this drill further, you can introduce other tasks - volley, chest trap or catch with your knees.

Can you think of any more to add?

Player
OF THE
Season

For the second year running, Troy Deeney took home both the Player of the Year and Players' Player of the Year trophies at the club's 2014/15 End of Season Awards Night.

The club captain's influence was vital as ever both on the pitch and off as the Hornets achieved automatic promotion to the Premier League, Deeney finishing Watford's top scorer with a 21-goal haul. Among the strikes were an impressive hat-trick against Fulham at Craven Cottage, as well as crucial goals against Wigan, Fulham, Bolton and Brighton in the second half of the season which saw Deeney further enhance his reputation as a match-winner in the Championship.

The Birmingham-born striker also firmly etched his name in the Watford history books, becoming the first player in the club's history to hit 20+ goals in three successive seasons - during 2012/13 he scored 20, and in 2013/14 he enjoyed a career-best 25-goal campaign. The 26-year-old was duly rewarded for his contributions with a new five-year contract ahead of the 2015/16 Premier League campaign. Signed on the eve of the 2010/11 season from Walsall for an initial £250,000, Deeney was often asked to perform a bustling wide midfield role early on into life at Vicarage Road, three goals from 20 starts not telling the full tale of a hard-working year of fast-tracked Championship learning and experience.

The sale of Marvin Sordell to Bolton in January 2012 proved a turning point in Deeney's on-pitch fortunes, the striker bagging 12 goals from 31 starts in 2011/12 - nine of which in the final three months of the season.

But Deeney's most memorable goal in Watford colours remains his final strike of 2012/13.

An astonishingly dramatic injury-time winner in the Play-Off Semi-Final with Leicester City, dispatched just moments after Manuel Almunia's double-save from an Anthony Knockaert penalty, was truly the stuff of Hornets folklore.

TROY DEENEY

WATFORD

Just as athletics records are broken,
as runners get faster and faster,
in football each generation of players
are faster, fitter and stronger than before.

Fitness FIRST

Clubs have more and more support staff, to provide everything a player will need to help him become the supreme athlete. These days, teams have fitness & conditioning coaches and nutritionists, who make sure every player is in the best physical shape he can be.

In pre-season, clubs carry out all kinds of tests on their players to monitor their progress and ensure each individual reaches and maintains peak fitness. A lot of work is done in the gym with weights, designed to make sure players have the strength not to be easily knocked off the ball and that they also possess the stamina to get through 90 minutes and not fade in the game's latter stages.

Of course, while fitness is essential, ultimately it is their ability that matters. Footballers like to train with the ball and work hard on their skills. A lot of drills are undertaken to develop and maintain each player's ability on the ball. Coaching staff also work on team play, formations and developing understandings on the pitch.

A large proportion of goals come from set-pieces, so teams work on not just taking them, but defending free-kicks, corners and throw ins. Every team has a specialist dead-ball expert who they rely on for these important moments in games. Some teams prefer to do man-for-man marking and some use the zonal approach. In man-for-man marking, every player has a responsibility to mark a particular opponent, while zonal marking means, every player has an area of the pitch that they have to defend.

Whichever system is used, it is important that players work hard in training, so that they are a fully fit and well organised unit, and can perform together, successfully as a team.

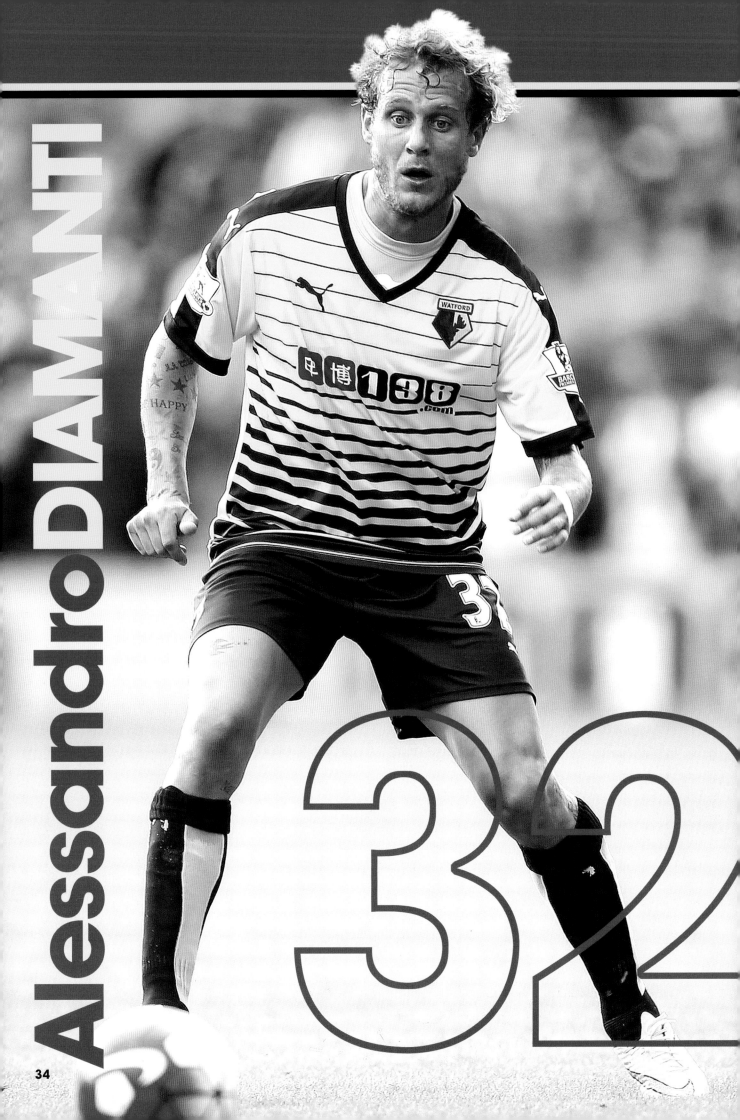

Alessandro **DIAMANTI**

32

Goal OF THE Season

WATFORD

The Hornets scored 91 goals on their way to gaining promotion to the Premier League, so it would take something spectacular to be crowned Goal of the Year, at the 2014/15 End of Season Awards Night.

With many strikes in contention, it was concluded that there wasn't one better than Almen Abdi's in early December 2014, in a 5-0 win over Fulham for the Golden Boys.

Other contenders included goals from Craig Cathcart, Troy Deeney and Odion Ighalo, but none came closer than the midfield maestro's just prior to the turn of the year. The Hornets star picked the ball up just outside the area, before turning and unleashing a powerful drive into the top corner, leaving Gábor Király with absolutely no chance of stopping it. The stunning goal was the fourth in Watford's 5-0 demolition of ten-man Fulham at Craven Cottage, in front of the Sky Sports cameras.

After slipping to four defeats in a row which saw the Golden Boys drop from the top of the Championship to seventh, the promotion bid was put back on track thanks to five of the best.

A hat-trick from the talismanic Troy Deeney, and a double from Swiss star Abdi, including the screamer, sealed the win for Slavisa Jokanovic's Hornets.

After picking up the prestigious award, Abdi spoke to Hornets Player about his wonder goal.

"First of all I have to be very thankful to everyone who voted for me. I don't remember too much about the goal, I just remember picking up the ball and then acting on instinct. I couldn't have hit it any better to be honest, I didn't thrash at the ball, and it ended up in the top corner. It was a great team performance that day too, so for the two to go together was something I was really happy with."

Can you identify the nicknames and match them to the Premier League club?

MANCHESTER UNITED · STOKE CITY · LEICESTER CITY · WEST HAM UNITED · NEWCASTLE UNITED · EVERTON · ARSENAL · SWANSEA CITY

A. CLUB:
   NICKNAME:

The Big Match

B. CLUB: NICKNAME:

C. CLUB: NICKNAME:

D. CLUB: NICKNAME:

E. CLUB: NICKNAME:

F. CLUB: NICKNAME:

G. CLUB: NICKNAME:

H. CLUB: NICKNAME:

Harry has some sums for you...

WATFORD

Using the squad numbers of Watford's players can you do the following sums?

Harry's Sums

Here's an example for you:

Obbi Oulare is number 10 and Miguel Britos is number 3 so Obbi Oulare X Miguel Britos is 30, because 10 X 3 = 30. You'll find the answers on page 62.

Etienne CAPOUE	+	Obbi OULARE	=	◯
Ikechi ANYA	+	Sebastian PRODL	=	◯
Steven BERGHUIS	+	Craig CATHCART	=	◯
Adlene GUEDIOURA	−	Troy DEENEY	=	◯
Ben WATSON	−	Almen ABDI	=	◯
Rene GILMARTIN	−	Valon BEHRAMI	=	◯
Joel EKSTRAND	X	Allan NYOM	=	◯
Lloyd DOYLEY	X	Miguel BRITOS	=	◯
Odion IGHALO	÷	Valon BEHRAMI	=	◯
Dennon LEWIS	÷	Rene GILMARTIN	=	◯

MEET YOUR RIVALS

MANCHESTER UNITED

GROUND: Old Trafford **CAPACITY:** 75,731
MANAGER: Louis van Gaal **NICKNAME:** The Red Devils
DID YOU KNOW: Manchester United have won the most League titles (twenty) of any English club, a joint record eleven FA Cups, four League Cups and a record twenty FA Community Shields.

NEWCASTLE UNITED

GROUND: St James' Park **CAPACITY:** 52,405
MANAGER: Steve McClaren **NICKNAME:** The Magpies
DID YOU KNOW: They have a fierce local rivalry with Sunderland, and the two clubs have contested the Tyne-Wear derby since 1898.

NORWICH CITY

GROUND: Carrow Road **CAPACITY:** 27,244
MANAGER: Alex Neil **NICKNAME:** The Canaries
DID YOU KNOW:
The fans' song "On the Ball, City"
is regarded as being the oldest football song in the world.

SOUTHAMPTON

GROUND: St Mary's Stadium **CAPACITY:** 32,689
MANAGER: Ronald Koeman **NICKNAME:** Saints
DID YOU KNOW: The club has been nicknamed the 'Saints' since its inception in 1885, due to its history as a church football team.

STOKE CITY

GROUND: Britannia Stadium **CAPACITY:** 27,743
MANAGER: Mark Hughes **NICKNAME:** The Potters
DID YOU KNOW: Founded as Stoke Ramblers in 1863, they are the second oldest pro football club in the world (after Notts County) and are one of the founder members of the Football League.

SUNDERLAND

GROUND: Stadium of Light **CAPACITY:** 49,000
MANAGER: Dick Advocaat **NICKNAME:** The Black Cats
DID YOU KNOW: Prior to the 2015/16 season, Sunderland had beaten arch-rivals Newcastle United in their last five league encounters.

SWANSEA CITY

GROUND: Liberty Stadium **CAPACITY:** 20,520
MANAGER: Garry Monk **NICKNAME:** The Swans
DID YOU KNOW: When Swansea City were promoted in 2011, the Swans became the first Welsh team to compete in the Premier League.

TOTTENHAM HOTSPUR

GROUND: White Hart Lane **CAPACITY:** 36,284
MANAGER: Mauricio Pochettino **NICKNAME:** Spurs
DID YOU KNOW: The club's Latin motto is 'Audere est Facere' - 'To Dare Is to Do'. Their long-standing rivalry with Arsenal is known as the North London derby.

WEST BROMWICH ALBION

GROUND: The Hawthorns **CAPACITY:** 26,850
HEAD COACH: Tony Pulis **NICKNAME:** The Baggies
DID YOU KNOW: Albion were one of the founding members of the Football League when it was formed in 1888.

WEST HAM UNITED

GROUND: The Boleyn Ground **CAPACITY:** 35,016
MANAGER: Slaven Bilic **NICKNAME:** The Hammers
DID YOU KNOW: This is West Ham's final season at the Boleyn Ground before they move to their new home.

TROY DEENEY

FAVOURITES

Animal? Sharks
Film? John Q
Colour? Red
Sweets? Haribo

Pizza topping? Chicken
Game? Stuck in the Mud
Actor? Will Smith
Actress? Scarlett Johansson
Song? Love and affections

Toughest player you have played against?
Kurt Zouma

Best moment of your career?
That goal against Leicester

Most interesting thing we don't know about you?
I'm currently studying business

Name three people, alive or dead, who you'd invite to your fantasy dinner party?
Will Smith, Tupac and Mike Tyson

Who do you most admire in football?
Ian Wright

Most annoying habit?
Clicking my knuckles

Theme tune?
Man's World - James Brown.

BERNARD MENSAH

FAVOURITES

Game? Football Manager
Actor? Damian Wayans
Actress? Tisha Campbell-Martin
Song? Who the Cap Fit, Bob Marley

Pizza topping? Pepperoni
Animal? Goat
Sweets? Skittles
Place? Home

Toughest player you have played against?
Nyron Nosworthy

Advice for young talent out there?
Hard work beats talent, when talent doesn't work hard

Most annoying habit?
Just being a pest!

Theme tune?
Batman theme tune

Funniest thing to have happened to you?
Came into training ground to find out that we were not actually training!

Name three people, alive or dead, who you'd invite to your fantasy dinner party?
James Brown, Kevin Hart and Yaya Sanogo

Most interesting thing we don't know about you?
I am the heir to the throne in a village in Ghana

TOMMIE HOBAN

FAVOURITES

Game? Call of Duty
Animal? Dolphin
Place? Mexico
Sweets? Crispy roll

Pizza topping? Ham
Film? Shawshank Redemption
Actor? Leonard Di Caprio
Actress? Margot Robbie
Song? Rockstar - Nickleback

Toughest player you have played against?
Didier Drogba

Who do you most admire in football?
On the pitch, John Terry

Theme tune?
Eye of the Tiger

Most annoying habit?
The way I eat

If you were on an island and could only bring three things, what would you bring?
Phone Charger, Phone and Water Filtration System

Most interesting thing we don't know about you?
If I wasn't a footballer, I would have been a doctor.

Name three people, alive or dead, who you'd invite to your fantasy dinner party?
Julius Cesar, Jesus and John Terry

Heurelho GOMES

Arguably the most popular player ever to wear Watford's colours, Blissett's goals earned him Vicarage Road records, international appearances and a £1m transfer to Italy.

In Watford's first season in the top division, Blissett scored 27 goals, which subsequently led to his move to AC Milan the following season. Wherever his career took him, Luther invariably came back to Watford, and was later Reserve Team Manager. In May 2002, he moved to York City to carry out a coaching role but later left that post and has since been involved in coaching strikers within the Football League while also trying his hand at non-League management.

LutherBLISSETT

Watford 1976-1992: 503 Games · 186 Goals

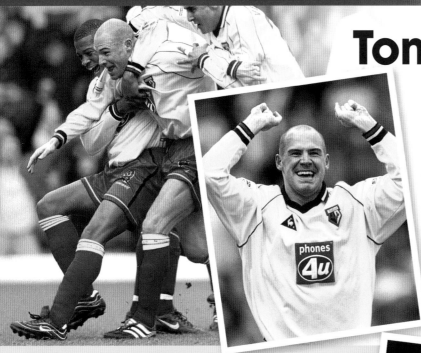

TommyMOONEY

Watford 1994-2001
288 Games · 63 Goals

Originally signed on-loan, Mooney was signed permanently in 1994, from Southend United. At first he struggled to play regularly in his preferred striker role, often deployed as a defender, but in 1999 he picked up his form and went on to be a key member of the side that reached the Premiership.

One of Watford's brightest moments in the top-flight was to come through Mooney, as his solitary goal in front of the Kop gave them a 1-0 victory over Liverpool. After spells across the Football League, including Birmingham, Swindon, Oxford, and Wycombe, Mooney retired from the game scoring over 200 goals in a 700+ game career.

RossJENKINS

Watford 1972-1983:
398 Games · 142 Goals

Ross Jenkins started his career at Crystal Palace, before joining Watford for a then club-record fee of £30,000. After struggling initially at Vicarage Road, Jenkins became a terrace hero as he played a major role in the success of the 1970s and 1980s.

After rejecting a move to Huddersfield in the summer of 1975, the Londoner went on to play an important role in the club's rise back to the top of English football. With the Golden Boys finishing second to Liverpool in the 1982/83 season, Jenkins left the club, joining Hong Kong side Eastern AA. The talismanic striker featured for the Hornets in all four divisions, netting 142 goals in just shy of 400 appearances for the club.

DRILLS: Attacking

Set up a square within shooting distance of your goal. Place a keeper in goal, and a defender inside the square.

You and the rest of your mates are attackers and should start at the other side of the square from the goal.

EASY

Dribble into the square and try to beat the defender and dribble out of the opposite side of the square.

If you successfully dribble through the square without losing the ball to the defender, finish with a shot on goal!

If you lose the ball to the defender or dribble out either side of the square, you must then switch places with the defender so that you are protecting the square and they become an attacker.

The next player in line can go as soon as a shot on goal is taken or the defender has won the ball.

HARD

You can make the square bigger to make it easier for the attackers or make the square smaller to make it easier for the defenders.

HARDER

You can make the square slightly larger and add a second defender so that the game becomes 2 v 1 and harder for the attacker.

To make shooting harder, move the square further away from the goal and encourage a longer shot.

The purpose of this drill is to focus on dribbling to beat a defender and finishing with a shot on goal.

Remember to take turns being in goal so that everyone gets a chance to play all positions!

WATFORD

Can you figure out the identity of these Watford stars?

WATFORD

A

B

E

who are yer?

44

ANSWERS ON PAGE 62

WATFORD

C

D

F

G

Etienne CAPOUE

29

WATFORD

Second half
OF THE SEASON

WATFORD

**WATFORD
V CHELSEA**

Who was Chelsea's
Player of the Year
last season?

24. ANSWER

**WATFORD
V MANCHESTER CITY**

Who was City's
top scorer
last season?

20. ANSWER

**TOTTENHAM HOTSPUR
V WATFORD**

Where do Spurs
play their
home games?

25. ANSWER

**SOUTHAMPTON
V WATFORD**

What is
Southampton's
famous anthem?

21. ANSWER

**SWANSEA CITY
V WATFORD**

Which company
manufactures
the Swans' kit?

22. ANSWER

**CRYSTAL PALACE
V WATFORD**

What is the
name of Palace's
home ground?

26. ANSWER

**WATFORD
V NEWCASTLE UNITED**

Nicknamed the Magpies,
what creatures are on
their club badge?

23. ANSWER

**WATFORD
V BOURNEMOUTH**

The Cherries were promoted
to the Premier League as
Championship top dogs last
season. True or false?

27. ANSWER

MANCHESTER UNITED V WATFORD

Manchester United have won 20 league titles, the most of any English club. True or false?

28. ANSWER

WATFORD V ASTON VILLA

Who are the Villans' fiercest rivals?

36. ANSWER

WATFORD V LEICESTER CITY

The Foxes got a new manager this season. Who is he?

29. ANSWER

ARSENAL V WATFORD

Who is Arsenal's current and longest serving manager?

32. ANSWER

LIVERPOOL V WATFORD

Name the Reds' club anthem.

37. ANSWER

WEST HAM UNITED V WATFORD

West Ham are leaving the Boleyn Ground at the and of the season. Where are they going?

30. ANSWER

WATFORD V EVERTON

With which team do Everton contest the Merseyside derby?

33. ANSWER

WEST BROMWICH ALBION V WATFORD

What are the names of Albion's mascots?

34. ANSWER

WATFORD V SUNDERLAND

Where was SAFC's home before the Stadium of Light?

38. ANSWER

WATFORD V STOKE CITY

Who was Stoke City's top scorer last season?

31. ANSWER

NORWICH CITY V WATFORD

In what year did the Canaries last lift the League Cup?

35. ANSWER

Tony Coton signed for Watford at the beginning of the 1984/85 season, and went on to appear over 230 times for the Golden Boys.

Signed from Birmingham as a 23–year-old, Coton had already earned himself a good reputation having made his Football League debut at the tender age of 19, but it was at the Hornets that he truly began to excel. Brought for £300,000 by Graham Taylor, Coton went on to win the prestigious Watford Player of the Year award a record three times. The last of these awards came in his final season in 1989/90, before his consistently excellent performances earned him a big money move to Manchester City.

Tony COTON

Alec CHAMBERLAIN

Signed from Sunderland for £40,000, Chamberlain is a goalkeeper with legendary status due to his true professionalism throughout his playing time at the club, which spanned over ten years.

Chamberlain was part of the club's rise to the Premiership and he picked up two Player of the Season awards as well - his heroics in the 1999 play-off semi-final with Birmingham City will live long in the memory for many supporters. A dedicated professional, he didn't have any problem winning over the fans after playing for rivals Luton Town between 1988 and 1993.The keeper now looks after the current crop of Academy goalkeepers at the club.

Steve SHERWOOD

Steve Sherwood is one of the most reliable goalkeepers in the club's history, having clocked up over 200 appearances for the Golden Boys in an 11-year spell.

It is no coincidence that Sherwood's spell with the club was also the most successful in Watford's history, having spent every season in Hertfordshire along with Graham Taylor between 1976 and 1987. During this period, Sherwood was a key part of the side that won promotion to Division 1, finished second in the English top flight the next season, qualified for European football and reached an FA Cup final. Perhaps not the most spectacular keeper in Watford's illustrious history, but Sherwood's reliable hands were a key feature in the most successful decade in the Hornets history.

DRILLS: Goalkeeping

WATFORD

Set up three cones in a large triangle. These become our three goals!

Make sure the triangle is big enough for the goalie to dive around in.

The goalie stands in the centre of the triangle and three shooters stand opposite the three goals at their 'penalty spots'.

This drill is very tiring for the keeper. Remember to swap positions so that everyone gets the chance to be in goal.

EASY

To start with, the shooters take it in turns to fire shots past the goalie - the goalie must work quickly to reposition himself for the next shot.

HARD

Players then start to fire shots more quickly. Just as the goalkeeper recovers from the last shot, the next player quickly shoots again.

HARDER

Change the order in which the shooters take their shots. Shooters shout their names in any order, to signal that they are going to shoot.

This keeps the goalie on his toes.

Also, be sure to try different shots - high, low, left foot, right foot, maybe even try chipping the ball over the keeper's head!

Can you match each of these crests to the Premier League club they belong too?

NORWICH CITY · WBA · LEICESTER CITY · WEST HAM UNITED · SUNDERLAND · LIVERPOOL · CRYSTAL PALACE · SWANSEA CITY

WATFORD

A. CLUB:

B. CLUB:

The Big Match

C. CLUB:

D. CLUB:

E. CLUB:

F. CLUB:

G. CLUB:

H. CLUB:

1892

Odion IGHALO

BEN WATSON

FAVOURITES

Game? Don't Play!
Actor? Daniel Craig
Animal? Hippo
Place? Dubai

Pizza topping? Meat
Film? Any James Bond!
Actress? Angelina Jolie
Song? Any Coldplay song
Colour? Yellow

What has been the best moment of your career?
Winning the FA Cup

Toughest player you have played against?
Yaya Toure

Who do you most admire in football?
Paul Scholes

Advice for young talent out there?
Work harder than those around you

Theme tune?
Oasis - Wonderwall

Name three people, alive or dead, who you'd invite to your fantasy dinner party?
Ed Sheeran, Ron Weasley and someone else ginger!

TEAM *Mates*

ALEX JAKUBIAK

FAVOURITES

Game? FIFA
Animal? Dog
Place? Vicarage Road
Sweets? Fruit Gum

Pizza topping? Pepperoni
Film? Wolf of Wall Street
Actor? Leonardo Di Caprio
Actress? Margot Robbie
Song? Cheerleader - OMI

Toughest player you have played against?
Lloyd Doyley

Best moment of your career?
Making my debut

Who do you most admire in football?
Cristiano Ronaldo

Advice for young talent out there?
Never give up

Most annoying habit?
Snoring

Theme tune?
Bad Boyz For Life

Name three people, alive or dead, who you'd invite to your fantasy dinner party?
Becks, Pele and Ronaldo

Most interesting thing we don't know about you?
I'm good at Ping Pong

JORELL JOHNSON

FAVOURITES

Game? FIFA
Actor? Will Smith
Animal? Dog
Place? Football pitch

Pizza topping? Pepperoni
Film? Focus
Actress? Mila Kunis
Sweets? Crispy roll
Colour? Red

Toughest player you have played against?
Troy Deeney

Who do you most admire in football?
The fans

Have you got any pre-match superstitions?
Left first, everything I do is done starting on the left

Most annoying habit?
I laugh at awkward times

Theme tune?
Here comes the boom by Nelly

Name three people, alive or dead, who you'd invite to your fantasy dinner party?
Becks, Messi and Ronaldo

Most interesting thing we don't know about you?
I can do impressions

Can you identify the
nine Hornets below?

A

B

C

Face Off!

D

E

F

G

H

I

WATFORD

2016
Predictions

OUR PREDICTION
FOR BARCLAYS
PREMIER LEAGUE
CHAMPIONS:

Chelsea

OUR PREDICTION FOR BARCLAYS
PREMIER LEAGUE RUNNERS UP:

Arsenal

YOUR PREDICTION:

YOUR PREDICTION:

OUR PREDICTION FOR BARCLAYS
PREMIER LEAGUE BOTTOM THREE:

Bournemouth, Aston Villa & WBA

YOUR PREDICTION:

Premier League

OUR PREDICTION FOR CHAMPIONSHIP WINNERS:

Derby County

YOUR PREDICTION:

League Cup

OUR PREDICTION FOR LEAGUE CUP WINNERS:

Manchester City

YOUR PREDICTION:

Championship

OUR PREDICTION FOR ALSO PROMOTED
TO THE BARCLAYS PREMIER LEAGUE:

Ipswich Town & Burnley

YOUR PREDICTION:

OUR PREDICTION FOR FA CUP WINNERS:

Watford

YOUR PREDICTION:

FACup

Jose Manuel JURADO

Start by juggling the ball with your feet

Kick it a little higher than normal to give you more time to complete the move

Lift the ball with the outside of your foot, putting a slight spin on it

Continue to bring your leg round and up over the ball

AROUND THE WORLD

Remember...

Finally...

...and continue to juggle the ball!

...that all this should be done in one fluid motion

...bring your foot back round to your starting position

We've set you a huge challenge for the new year! Every month there are two tasks to complete

2016 Challenge

WATFORD

JANUARY

- [X] Do **25** keepy-uppies.
- [X] Come up with a new Hornets chant!

FEBRUARY

- [X] Take a selfie at a Premier League Stadium.
- [X] **LEARN A NEW TRICK Around the world!**

NUTMEG

- [X] **NUTMEG** your best mate!
- [X] Get an autograph from a Watford star player.

APRIL

- [X] Do **50** keepy-uppies.
- [X] Take a selfie with a Hornet star.

MARCH

MAY

- [X] WORK ON YOUR FITNESS **Run 1 mile!**
- [X] **Lob the keeper.**

60

Have you got what it takes?

JUNE

☐ **LEARN A NEW TRICK**
Catch the ball on the back your neck!

☒ Do your bit for charity - set up a sponsored event with your mates.

JULY

☒ KEEPY-UPPY CHALLENGE
10 with a...
tennis ball!

☒ WORK ON YOUR FITNESS
Run 3 miles!

AUGUST

☒ Take a selfie with a Watford legend.

☒ **Do 75 keepy-uppies.**

SEPTEMBER

☒ KEEPY-UPPY CHALLENGE
10 on your...
head!

☒ Try out for your school footie team.

OCTOBER

☒ Shake Harry the Hornet by the hand.

☒ **Take a selfie with Quique Sánchez Flores**

NOVEMBER

☒ WORK ON YOUR FITNESS
Run 5 miles!

☒ **Blast a penalty in off the underside of the crossbar.**

DECEMBER

☒ **Do 100 keepy-uppies.**

☒ **Start a chant at the match.**

61

WATFORD

PAGE 22: THE BIG MATCH - MASCOTS

A. Samson the Cat, Sunderland. B. Captain Canary, Norwich City. C. Fred the Red, Manchester United. D. Barney Owl, Sheffield Wednesday. E. Kop Cat, Leeds United. F. Beau Brummie, Birmingham City. I. Gunnersaurus, Arsenal. H. Hammerhead, West Ham Utd.

PAGE 24: CROWD PLEASERS

Benedict Cumberbatch, Keira Knightley, Idris Elba, Emma Watson and Andrew Lincoln.

PAGE 26 · 1ST HALF OF THE SEASON

1. Tim Howard. 2. A throstle (Song Thrush). 3. 1976. 4. Santiago, Chile. 5. True. 6. Mike Ashley. 7. The Eagles. 8. Maxim Demin. 9. Gold. 10. Staffordshire. 11. I'm forever blowing bubbles. 12. False. They are known as the Foxes. 13. Newton Heath. 14. Paul Lambert. 15. Russell Martin. 16. Dick Advocaat. 17. Seven. 18. 41,798. 19. To dare is to do.

PAGE 36: THE BIG MATCH - NICKNAMES

A. Manchester United, The Red Devils. B. West Ham United, The Hammers. C. Leicester City, The Foxes. D. Stoke City, The Potters. E. Swansea City, The Swans. F. Newcastle United, The Magpies. G. Arsenal, The Gunners. H. Everton, The Toffees.

PAGE 37: HARRY'S SUMS

1. Dennon Lewis, 9. 2. Bernard Mensah, 26. 3. Josh Doherty, 35. 4. Valon Behrami, 8. 5. Heurelho Gomes, 1. 6. Sebastien Prodl, 5. 7. Lloyd Doyley, 12. 8. Alex Jakubiak, 36. 9. Miguel Britos, 3. 10. Miguel Britos, 3.

PAGE 44: WHO ARE YER?

A. Allan Nyom. B. Alessandro Diamanti. C. Jose Manuel Jurado. D. Alon Behrami. E. Troy Deeney. F. Sebastian Prodl. G. Ben Watson.

PAGE 48 · 2ND HALF OF THE SEASON

20. Sergio Aguero. 21. When the Saints Go Marching In. 22. adidas. 23. Seahorses. 24. Eden Hazard. 25. White Hart Lane. 26. Selhurst Park. 27. True. 28. True. 29. Claudio Ranieri. 30. Queen Elizabeth Olympic Park. 31. Mame Biram Diouf. 32. Arsene Wenger. 33. Liverpool. 34. Baggie Bird and Albi. 35. 1985. 36. Birmingham City. 37. You'll Never Walk Alone. 38. Roker Park.

PAGE 52: THE BIG MATCH - CRESTS

A. West Ham United. B. Crystal Palace. C. Sunderland. D. Norwich City. E. Leicester City. F. West Bromwich Albion. G. Swansea City. H. Liverpool.

PAGE 55: FACE OFF!

A. Deeney. B. Behrami. C. Johnson. D. Abdi. E. Watson. F. Britos. G. Prodl. H. Gomes. I. Paredes.